Design for Six Sigma (DFSS)

By Ade Asefeso MCIPS MBA

Second Edition

ISBN-13: 978-1499775440

ISBN-10: 149977544X

Publisher: AA Global Sourcing Ltd
Website: http://www.aaglobalsourcing.com

Table of Contents

Disclaimer

This publication is designed to provide competent and reliable information regarding the subject matter covered. However, it is sold with the understanding that the author and publisher are not engaged in rendering professional advice. The authors and publishers specifically disclaim any liability that is incurred from the use or application of contents of this book.

If you purchased this book without a cover you should be aware that this book may have been stolen property and reported as "unsold and destroyed" to the publisher. In this case neither the author nor the publisher has received any payment for this "stripped book."

Dedication

This book is dedicated to the hundreds of thousands of incredible souls in the world who have weathered through the up and down of recent recession.

To my family and friends who seems to have been sent here to teach me something about who I am supposed to be. They have nurtured me, challenged me, and even opposed me.... But at every juncture has taught me!

This book is dedicated to my lovely boys, Thomas, Michael and Karl. Teaching them to manage their finance will give them the lives they deserve. They have taught me more about life, presence, and energy management than anything I have done in my life.

Chapter 1: Introduction

Design for Six Sigma (DFSS), or the Six Sigma DMADV process (Define, Measure, Analyze, Design, Verify), is an improvement system used to develop new processes or products at Six Sigma quality levels. It also can be employed if a current process requires more than just incremental improvement. It is executed by Six Sigma Green Belts and Six Sigma Black Belts, and overseen by Six Sigma Master Black Belts.

The best Six Sigma projects begin not inside the business but outside it, focused on answering the question, how can we make the customer more competitive?
Jack Welch

Since you are reading this book, you are probably familiar with at least the basics of Six Sigma. So, we can review briefly before getting into Design for Six Sigma.

Six Sigma is a revolutionary business process geared toward dramatically reducing organizational inefficiencies that translates into bottom-line profitability. It started in the 1980s at Motorola; then, organizations such as GE, Allied Signal, and Seagate worked with the initiative during the 1990s and made it the most successful business initiative of the era.

Key to the Six Sigma methodology of the 1990s is a five step Process — Define, Measure, Analyze,

Improve, and Control (DMAIC). By systematically applying these steps (with the appropriate tools), practitioners of this approach have been able to save a lot of money.

The basis of Six Sigma is measuring a process in terms of defects. The statistical concept of six sigma means your processes are working nearly perfectly, delivering only 3.4 defects per million opportunities (DPMO). As you know from your experience with Six Sigma, Sigma (the Greek letter σ) is a statistical term that measures standard deviation. In the context of management, it's used to measure defects in the outputs of a process and show how far the process deviates from perfection.

Design for Six Sigma (DFSS)

Design for Six Sigma (DFSS) is a separate and emerging business-process management methodology related to traditional Six Sigma. While the tools and order used in Six Sigma require a process to be in place and functioning, DFSS has the objective of determining the needs of customers and the business, and driving those needs into the product solution so created. DFSS is relevant to the complex system/product synthesis phase, especially in the context of unprecedented system development. It is process generation in contrast with process improvement.

DMADV, Define – Measure – Analyze – Design – Verify, is sometimes synonymously referred to as DFSS. The traditional DMAIC (Define – Measure –

Analyze – Improve – Control) Six Sigma process, as it is usually practiced, which is focused on evolutionary and continuous improvement manufacturing or service process development, usually occurs after initial system or product design and development have been largely completed. DMAIC Six Sigma as practiced is usually consumed with solving existing manufacturing or service process problems and removal of the defects and variation associated with defects. On the other hand, DFSS (or DMADV) strives to generate a new process where none existed, or where an existing process is deemed to be inadequate and in need of replacement. DFSS aims to create a process with the end in mind of optimally building the efficiencies of Six Sigma methodology into the process before implementation; traditional Six Sigma seeks for continuous improvement after a process already exists.

Chapter 2: Design for Six Sigma and Lean Manufacturing

After initial success, Six Sigma methodology has become the strategy of many corporations. Before the advent of Six Sigma, as discovered by Motorola, initiatives such as design for manufacturability (DFM), cycle time reduction (or lean manufacturing) and waste reduction existed. Six Sigma methodologies have evolved to incorporate DFM and lean manufacturing. What is interesting to note is that DFM and lean manufacturing have become post-Six Sigma initiatives, instead of prerequisites for implementing Six Sigma successfully.

Quality assurance has evolved from end-of-line inspection (product inspection) to online inspection, to process control (control charts), and to off-line inspection (DFM), quality management systems (ISO 9000) and Six Sigma (dramatic improvement).

During this evolution, many tools, techniques and systems have been invented. Commonly known systems are pareto charts, cause-effect diagrams, control charts, design of experiments, Taguchi methods, zero defects, quality function deployment, Malcolm Baldrige National Quality Award Guidelines, Triz (Russian methods for systematic innovation), ISO 9000, QS-9000 and Six Sigma. Names like Walter Shewhart, Ed Deming, J.M. Juran, Armond Feigennbaum and Phil Crosby are legends in the quality assurance industry. However, Six Sigma was invented at Motorola within a framework that included DFM and lean manufacturing.

DFM is achieved through concurrent design of product and processes. Design for Six Sigma uses an integrated approach to design so that the product is manufacturable at the highest quality and lowest cost and satisfies all of the customer's requirements. DFM is important to implement because the majority of manufacturing defects occur due to design-related issues. The success in creating a manufacturable product depends upon clearly defined product goals reflecting physical and functional requirements of the customer.

Products designed for Six Sigma using design for manufacturability processes will allow the following:
1. Virtually defect-free or robust product design
2. Waste-free manufacturing
3. 100 percent usable purchased parts
4. Minimal maintenance and service
5. Total customer satisfaction.

In a design for Six Sigma environment, the product design team works with a cross functional team consisting of members from marketing, sales, quality, manufacturing, purchasing and even customers.

An excellent measure of a product designed for Six Sigma performance is Cp that is defined as follows:
1. Design tolerance (Upper spec. limit – Lower spec. limit)
2. Cp = Process capability (6 σ)

If the Cp is equal to or greater than 2.0, the product design can be considered a Six Sigma design because, when transferred to production, it will most likely yield 99.9996 percent for each customer's critical characteristics.

For Six Sigma designs, the product design team should focus on the following considerations:
1. Fewest number of parts
2. Parts of known capability
3. Maximum design tolerances
4. Maximum operating margins
5. Minimal overstress.

The inventor of Six Sigma methodology at Motorola, Bill Smith, has stated that parts designed to the target conditions, with the above considerations and operating under normal conditions without overstress, will never fail.

Design for Six Sigma will also consider using tools such as quality function deployment for developing best-in-class products; failure modes and effects analysis (FMEA); creative methods such as Triz; design for assembly; simulation; design of experiments for optimization and Taguchi methods for robust designs.

Lean manufacturing is a way to specify value, arrange value-creating actions in the optimum sequence, conduct these activities without interruption and improve continually. Lean thinking is a way to do more with fewer resources to provide customers exactly what they want. The value is defined in terms of specific products with specific capabilities offered at a specific price to a customer. One identifies the value stream as a set of specific actions required to create value. Identifying the value stream for each product or service is a key step in lean thinking.

Typically, the actions in the value stream can be grouped in one of the three categories:
1. Actions creating value
2. Actions creating value but unavoidable immediately
3. Actions creating value and avoidable immediately.

Having identified the value stream, the wasteful steps are eliminated and the remaining value-creating steps flow. Lean thinking can be considered to be out-of the-box thinking.

Nothing is taken for granted. Every step is questionable. One of the opportunities for change is reducing the batch size. Having a large batch size is a natural inclination for high-volume producers to justify longer set-up times. Lean thinking challenges the batch size by focusing on reduction in set-up time. Batch size impacts purchasing quantities, maintenance, set-up time, material flow and quality improvement.

One of the measurements of lean manufacturing is inventory levels. Inventory is a good measure of manufacturing woes, because a natural company reaction is to build more or buy more just in case of a shortage. Suddenly, the cost of carrying the inventory starts eating up the profits.

Managing inventory is like managing the material river, where the volume of water is dependent on the length, depth and width of the river. Similarly, in a manufacturing operation, inventory level is dependent on the number of process steps (length), unique part counts in designs (width) and organizational policies (depth). When one starts reducing the inventory level, the rocks, or the problems, start to appear.
Continual improvement at a dramatic rate is a critical part of sustaining lean operations.

For parts manufactured with lean manufacturing and Six Sigma design, manufacturing engineers should focus on the following considerations:
1. Documentation
   a. Product design documentation
   b. Process manufacturing instructions
   c. Inspection and test procedures
   d. Repair and rework instructions
   e. Handling of nonconforming material
2. Processes of known capability
3. Simple and shortest process flow
4. Process reproducibility
5. Organizational policies.

Products designed for Six Sigma and built with lean thinking will be manufactured in a pull system and with virtual perfection. Ultimately, an organization's goal is to produce the highest quality product at the lowest cost and minimal waste. In such an environment, endless improvement is realized using kaizen (continual), as well as kaikaku (dramatic), methods.

Chapter 3: DFSS as an Approach to Design

DFSS seeks to avoid manufacturing/service process problems by using advanced Voice of the Customer techniques and proper systems engineering techniques to avoid process problems at the outset (i.e., fire prevention). When combined, these methods obtain the proper needs of the customer, and derive engineering system parameter requirements that increase product and service effectiveness in the eyes of the customer. This yields products and services that provide greater customer satisfaction and increased market share.

These techniques also include tools and processes to predict, model and simulate the product delivery system (the processes/tools, personnel and organization, training, facilities, and logistics to produce the product/service) as well as the analysis of the developing system life cycle itself to ensure customer satisfaction with the proposed system design solution. In this way, DFSS is closely related to systems engineering, operations research (solving the Knapsack problem), systems architecture and concurrent engineering.

DFSS is largely a design activity requiring specialized tools including: quality function deployment (QFD), axiomatic design, TRIZ, Design for X, design of experiments (DOE), Taguchi methods, tolerance design, Robustification and Response Surface Methodology for a single or multiple response optimization. While these tools are sometimes used in the classic DMAIC Six Sigma process, they are uniquely used by DFSS to analyze new and unprecedented systems/products. A graphical flowchart of common DFSS tools can be seen at DFSS Roadmap. An additional roadmap for the metrics that may be utilized to deploy DFSS on a company-wide level may be seen at DFSS Metrics.

Arguments over the separation of DFSS from DMAIC / Six Sigma or Lean

Six Sigma Proponents of DMAIC and Lean techniques might claim that DFSS falls under the general rubric of Six Sigma or Lean Six Sigma. It is often seen that the tools used for DFSS techniques vary widely from those used for DMAIC Six Sigma. In particular, DMAIC practitioners often use new or existing mechanical drawings and manufacturing process instructions as the originating information to perform their analysis, while DFSS practitioners often use system simulations and parametric system design/analysis tools to predict both cost and performance of candidate system architectures. While it can be claimed that two processes are similar, in practice the working medium differs enough so that DFSS requires different tool sets in order to perform its system design tasks. DMAIC Six Sigma may still be used during depth-first plunges into the system architecture analysis and for "back end" Six Sigma processes; DFSS provides system design processes used in front-end complex system designs.

18

Similarities with other methods

Arguments about what makes DFSS different from Six Sigma demonstrate the similarities between DFSS and other established engineering practices such as Probabilistic design and design for quality. In general Six Sigma with its DMAIC roadmap focuses on improvement of an existing process or processes. DFSS focuses on the creation of new value with inputs from customers, suppliers and business needs. While traditional Six Sigma may also use those inputs, the focus is again on improvement and not design of some new product or system. It also shows the engineering background of DFSS. However, like other methods developed in engineering, there is no theoretical reason why DFSS can't be used in areas outside of engineering.

Chapter 4: DFSS, Applied to Software Engineering

Historically, although the first successful Design for Six Sigma projects in 1989 and 1991 predate establishment of the DMAIC process improvement process, Design for Six Sigma (DFSS) is accepted in part because Six Sigma organisations found that they could not optimise products past three or four Sigma without fundamentally redesigning the product, and because improving a process or product after launch is considered less efficient and effective than designing in quality. 'Six Sigma' levels of performance have to be 'built-in'.

DFSS for Software is essentially a non superficial modification of "classical DFSS" since the character and nature of software is different from other fields of engineering. The methodology describes the detailed process for successfully applying DFSS methods and tools throughout the Software Product Design, covering the overall Software Development life cycle; Requirements, Architecture, Design, Implementation, Integration, Optimization, Verification and Validation (RADIOV). The methodology explains how to build predictive statistical models for software reliability and robustness and shows how simulation and analysis techniques can be combined with structural design and architecture methods to effectively produce software and information systems at Six Sigma levels. DFSS in Software acts as a glue to blend the classical modelling techniques of software engineering such as

OOD or ERD with statistical, predictive models and simulation techniques. The methodology provides Software Engineers with practical tools for measuring and predicting the quality attributes of the software product and also enables them to include software in system reliability models.

Chapter 5: Where Did the Name "Six Sigma" Come from?

In my recollection, two recurring questions have dominated the field of six sigma. The first inquiry can be described by the global question. Why 6s and not some other level of capability? The second inquiry is more molecular. It can be summarized by the question; Where does the 1.5s shift factor come from and why 1.5 versus some other magnitude.

At the onset of six sigma in 1985, an engineer by the name of Bill Smith originates the six sigma concept in 1984. At that time, he suggested Motorola should require 50 percent design margins for all of its key product performance specifications. Statistically speaking, such a "safety margin" is equivalent to a 6 sigma level of capability.

When considering the performance tolerance of a critical design feature, he believed a 25 percent "cushion" was not sufficient for absorbing a sudden shift in process centring. Bill believed the typical shift was on the order of 1.5s (relative to the target value). In other words, a four sigma level of capability would normally be considered sufficient, if centred. However, if the process centre was somehow knocked off its central location (on the order of 1.5s), the initial capability of 4s would be degraded to 4.0s − 1.5s = 2.5s. Of course, this would have a consequential impact on defects. In turn, a sudden increase in defects would have an adverse effect on reliability. As should be apparent, such a domino effect would continue straight up the value chain.

Regardless of the shift magnitude, those of us working this issue fully recognized that the initial estimate of capability will often erode over time in a "very natural way" thereby increasing the expected rate of product defects (when considering a protracted period of production). Extending beyond this, we concluded that the product defect rate was highly correlated to the long-term process capability, not the short-term capability. Of course, such conclusions were predicated on the statistical analysis of empirical data gathered on a wide array of electronic devices.

Thus, we come to understand three things. First, we recognized that the instantaneous reproducibility of a critical-to-quality characteristic is fully dependent on the "goodness of fit" between the operating bandwidth of the process and the corresponding bandwidth of the performance specification. Second, the quality of that interface can be substantively and consequentially disturbed by process centring error. Of course, both of these factors profoundly impact long-term capability. Third, we must seek to qualify our critical processes at a 6s level of short-term capability if we are to enjoy a long-term capability of 4s.

By further developing these insights through applied research, we were able to greatly extend our understanding of the many statistical connections between such things as design margin, process capability, defects, field reliability, customer satisfaction, and economic success.

Chapter 6: Six Sigma Evolution Clarified

I would like to use this book to clarify the evolution of six sigma since this seems to be a lively topic of conversation among many practitioners (even cartoonists!) these days.

The roots of six sigma as a measurement standard can be traced back to Carl Frederick Gauss (1777-1855) who introduced the concept of the normal curve. Six sigma as a measurement standard in product variation can be traced back to the 1920's when Walter Shewhart showed that three sigma from the mean is the point where a process requires correction. Many measurement standards (Cpk, Zero Defects, and so on) later came on the scene but credit for coining the term "six sigma" goes to a Motorola engineer named Bill Smith as mentioned in the earlier chapter of this book (six sigma is a federally registered trademark of Motorola).

In the late 1970's, Dr. Mikel Harry, a senior staff engineer at Motorola's Government Electronics Group (GEG), began to experiment with problem solving through statistical analysis. Using his methodology, GEG began to show dramatic results – GEG's products were being designed and produced faster and more cheaply. Subsequently, Dr. Harry began to formulate a method for applying six sigma throughout Motorola. His work culminated in a paper titled "The Strategic Vision for Accelerating Six Sigma within Motorola." He was later appointed head of the

Motorola Six Sigma Research Institute and became the driving force behind six sigma.

Dr. Mikel Harry and Richard Schroeder, an ex-Motorola executive, were responsible for creating the unique combination of change management and data-driven methodologies that transformed six sigma from a simple quality measurement tool to the breakthrough business excellence philosophy it is today. They had the charisma and the ability to educate and engage business leaders such as Bob Galvin of Motorola, Larry Bossidy of AlliedSignal (now Honeywell), and Jack Welch of GE. Together, Harry and Schroeder elevated six sigma from the shop floor to the boardroom with their drive and innovative ideas regarding entitlement, breakthrough strategy, sigma levels, and the roles for deployment of Black Belts, Master Black Belts, and Champions. In effect, they created a business revolution that continues to challenge the thinking of executives, managers and employees alike. Their strategies and tools have been perfected through the years by Six Sigma Academy.

In brief, their contribution was the unique combination of business leadership plus quality and process improvement tools and techniques which made it possible for leaders to recognize the value of six sigma, not just as a tool for operational efficiency, but as an enterprise wide business strategy with direct bottom line impact.

Having said all that, I believe every six sigma practitioner, consulting firm, and black belt has contributed to the evolution of six sigma. We should therefore focus our time and resources, not on diatribes about who can claim credit for six sigma, but rather on continuously improving upon the strategies and tactics to achieve breakthrough results in business excellence. For example, six sigma has been indisputably successful in eliminating waste, reducing variance and increasing productivity and profits. But its potential to create new business models for growth and innovation is barely tapped. I urge all of us to take six sigma to the next level by being thought leaders inspiring creativity and originality in our successors, instead of simply regurgitating what others have said before us. Doing so will ensure six sigma will become the global standard for conducting business, not just another management trend doomed to fall by the wayside.

There is a hill to scale ahead of us, and enough oxygen for everyone. It is incumbent upon all of us to blaze a trail toward the next frontier of six sigma and demonstrate the leadership businesses are clamouring for.

Chapter 7: Design for Six Sigma (DFSS) Versus DMAIC

One of the most confusing issues associated with someone saying "I'm using Six Sigma" has to do with what methodology they are actually using. A majority of the time they are using the DMAIC methodology, because they have existing processes that are wasting resources (hence the big savings you've heard about at GE, Honeywell and others over the past years). The remaining minority of Six Sigma practitioners are using a Design For Six Sigma (DFSS) approach to design a new product for Six Sigma quality.

What is DMAIC?

DMAIC refers to a data-driven quality strategy for improving processes, and is an integral part of the company's Six Sigma Quality Initiative. DMAIC is an acronym for five interconnected phases: Define, Measure, Analyze, Improve, and Control.

Each step in the cyclical DMAIC Process is required to ensure the best possible results. The process steps:
1. Define the Customer, their Critical to Quality (CTQ) issues, and the Core Business Process involved.
2. Define who customers are, what their requirements are for products and services, and what their expectations are.
3. Define project boundaries - the stop and start of the process.

4. Define the process to be improved by mapping the process flow.
5. Measure the performance of the Core Business Process involved.
6. Develop a data collection plan for the process.
7. Collect data from many sources to determine types of defects and metrics.
8. Compare to customer survey results to determine shortfall.
9. Analyze the data collected and process map to determine root causes of defects and opportunities for improvement.
10. Identify gaps between current performance and goal performance.
11. Prioritize opportunities to improve.
12. Identify sources of variation.
13. Improve the target process by designing creative solutions to fix and prevent problems.
14. Create innovate solutions using technology and discipline.
15. Develop and deploy implementation plan
16. Control the improvements to keep the process on the new course.

Prevent reverting back to the "old way"
1. Require the development, documentation and implementation of an ongoing monitoring plan.
2. Institutionalize the improvements through the modification of systems and structures staffing, training, incentives.

When most people refer to Six Sigma, they are in fact referring to the DMAIC methodology. The DMAIC methodology should be used when a product or process is in existence at your company but is not meeting customer specification or is not performing adequately.

The DMAIC methodology is almost universally recognized and defined as comprising of the following five phases: Define, Measure, Analyze, Improve and Control. In some businesses, only four phases (Measure, Analyze, Improve and Control) are used; in this case the Define deliverables are then considered pre-work for the project or are included within the Measure phase. I have even heard of DMAIIC, where the first I stands for Improve and the second I stands for Implement.

What is DFSS?

DFSS is the acronym for Design For Six Sigma. Unlike the DMAIC methodology, the phases or steps of DFSS are not universally recognized or defined; almost every company or training organization will define DFSS differently. Many times a company will implement DFSS to suit their business, industry and culture; other times they will implement the version of DFSS used by the consulting company assisting in the deployment. Because of this, DFSS is more of an approach than a defined methodology.

DFSS is used to design or re-design a product or service from the ground up. The expected process Sigma level for a DFSS product or service is at least

33

4.5 (no more than approximately 1 defect per thousand opportunities), but can be 6 Sigma or higher depending the product. Producing such a low defect level from product or service launch means that customer expectations and needs (CTQs) (Critical To Quality) must be completely understood before a design can be completed and implemented.

One popular Design for Six Sigma methodology is called DMADV, and retains the same number of letters, number of phases, and general feel as the DMAIC acronym. It rolls off the tongue (duh-mad-vee) in the same fashion as DMAIC (duh-may-ick).

The five phases of DMADV are defined as: Define, Measure, Analyze, Design and Verify.
1. Define the project goals and customer (internal and external) requirements.
2. Measure and determine customer needs and specifications; benchmark competitors and industry.
3. Analyze the process options to meet the customer needs.
4. Design (detailed) the process to meet the customer needs.
5. Verify the design performance and ability to meet customer needs.

There are a few other "flavours" of DFSS that you might be interested to know about:
DCCDI
IDOV
DMEDI

DCCDI is being popularized by Geoff Tennant and is defined as Define, Customer, Concept, Design and Implement. You can see that there are many similarities between these phases and the DMADV phases.

1. Define the project goals.
2. Customer analysis is completed.
3. Concept ideas are developed, reviewed and selected.
4. Design is performed to meet the customer and business specifications.
5. Implementation is completed to develop and commercialize the product/service.

IDOV is a well known design methodology, especially in the manufacturing world. The IDOV acronym is defined as Identify, Design, Optimize and Validate.

1. Identify the customer and specifications (CTQs).
2. Design translates the customer CTQs into functional requirements and into solution alternatives. A selection process whittles down the list of solutions to the "best" solution.
3. Optimize uses advanced statistical tools and modelling to predict and optimize the design and performance.
4. Validate makes sure that the design you've developed will meet the customer CTQs.

DMEDI is being taught by PricewaterhouseCoopers and stands for Define, Measure, Explore, Develop and Implement. I am sure you won't have much trouble identifying the main objectives in each of these phases based on the title of each phase.

As you can see, the DFSS approach can utilize any of the many possible methodologies. The fact is that all of these DFSS methodologies use the same advanced design tools (Quality Function Deployment, Failure Modes and Effects Analysis, benchmarking, Design of Experiments, simulation, statistical optimization, error proofing, Robust Design, etc.). Each methodology primarily differs in the name of each phase and the number of phases (and, of course, the acronym).

How do you decide which DFSS methodology to use? If you're hiring a consulting company to help with your deployment, use their methodology as their training materials will be tailored around it. If you are implementing DFSS on your own, any of the DFSS books available should get you moving in the right direction. In any case, following a detailed DFSS methodology will help you achieve high quality levels for new products and services. If you are interested in improving your existing products or services, DMAIC is a more appropriate methodology to use.

DMAIC versus DMADV

We know that everything in business is a process, right? Sales people have a list of companies and contacts that they work in a certain fashion to produce a sale, production receives an order and schedules the manufacturing, product is built, packaged, shipped and invoiced. When the packing department has a problem with their process, though, should they fix it with a DMAIC or DMADV (also referred to as DFSS) type project?

The Similarities of DMAIC and DMADV

Let's first look at the DMAIC and DMADV methodologies and talk about how they're alike. DMAIC and DMADV are both:

1. Six Sigma methodologies used to drive defects to less than 3.4 per million opportunities.
2. Data intensive solution approaches. Intuition has no place in Six Sigma; only cold, hard facts.
3. Implemented by Green Belts, Black Belts and Master Black Belts.
4. Ways to help meet the business/financial bottom-line numbers.
5. Implemented with the support of a champion and process owner.

The Differences of DMAIC and DMADV

DMAIC and DMADV sound very similar. The acronyms even share the first three letters. But that is about where the similarities stop!

DMAIC

1. Define the project goals and customer (internal and external) deliverables.
2. Measure the process to determine current performance.
3. Analyze and determine the root cause(s) of the defects.

4. Improve the process by eliminating defects.
5. Control future process performance.

When to Use DMAIC

The DMAIC methodology, instead of the DMADV methodology, should be used when a product or process is in existence at your company but is not meeting customer specification or is not performing adequately.

On the other hand DMADV

1. Define the project goals and customer (internal and external) deliverables.
2. Measure and determine customer needs and specifications.
3. Analyze the process options to meet the customer needs.
4. Design (detailed) the process to meet the customer needs.
5. Verify the design performance and ability to meet customer needs.

When to Use DMADV

The DMADV methodology, instead of the DMAIC methodology, should be used when; a product or process is not in existence at your company and one needs to be developed or the existing product or process exists and has been optimized (using either DMAIC or not) and still does not meet the level of customer specification or Six Sigma level.

"I Thought It Was a DMAIC, but It Turned Out to Be a DMADV!"

Occasionally a project is scoped as a DMAIC for incremental process improvement when it really required a DMADV methodology improvement. And it was a month into the project that you realized this!

Do not be discouraged about the work you put into the DMAIC because;
1. It has happened to more businesses than just yours.
2. You understand the process at a much greater detail than you did initially.
3. You were able to practice not just DMAIC skills but also DMADV!

Pick yourself up, dust yourself off and re-craft your define piece of the project so you can begin with a fresh look at the project and solutions. You never know what insights you will have now that you may not have been aware of before.

Chapter 8: DMAIC and DFSS Roadmaps: How to Connect and Integrate?

The roadmap has always been an important part of Six Sigma. It lays out the thought process for teams and leaders, and distinguishes the methodology from a parade of tools. With the original "Six Steps to Six Sigma" and then "Define Measure Analyze Improve Control" (DMAIC) as the improvement roadmap, plus the addition of Design for Six Sigma (DFSS), practitioners have evolved and expanded their view of how the steps and tools fit together and deliver results.

To make things interesting, DFSS is a lot less standard around the world than DMAIC. Roadmaps like "Define Measure Analyze Design Verify" (DMADV), "Invent/Innovate Develop Optimize Verify" (I2DOV) and "Concept Design Optimize Verify (CDOV) are similar in spirit, but with differences in nuance and detail. Add to this the common desire to map in other initiatives, like Lean and Business Process Management, and it's easy to see why companies sometimes think about rationalizing and perhaps simplifying their roadmap view.

While there are numerous coexistence and integration questions, a combined core DMAIC-DFSS roadmap is possible.

How to Deal with Two Roadmaps?

Many companies begin their Six Sigma work with DMAIC problem-solving and improvement. This makes sense as DMAIC brings rapid improvement to existing processes quickly returning significant dollars to the bottom line. Because DMAIC projects often point to problem root causes in the design of products or processes, interest in DFSS often develops in connection with improvement work. Thus leaders may find themselves struggling to manage two Six Sigma approaches and roadmaps.

In a world where "innovate and design" are naturally separated from "improvement work," two roadmaps may work just fine. In many real-world cases, though, design is often interwoven with existing products and processes, and improvement often means revisiting fundamental design. In those situations, the project teams, Belts and Champions can waste energy worrying, "Is this a DMAIC or DFSS project?"

The Appeal and Challenge in Integrating DMAIC and DFSS

When a company feels that too much time is being spent sweating out the distinctions between DMAIC and DFSS, it may move to integrate and simplify things. Experienced Six Sigma practitioners may notice that the thought processes have some parallels, especially in the Define and Control phases. While it is tempting, and even possible, to integrate the approaches in new and creative ways, it is best to use some common approaches with an eye toward caution. Integrating the roadmaps requires special attention to the subtle ways they are different.

Being Well-Armed with Insight

All practitioners appreciate that roadmaps are needed to guide the work in Six Sigma, and that there is an understandable need to simplify and integrate when their complexity starts to get in the way. While considering a "branched" and a "parallel" approach to integrating DMAIC and DFSS, one must be armed with as much insight at possible before deciding what is best in their particular environment.

Chapter 9: Design for Six Sigma – IDOV Methodology

Design for Six Sigma (DFSS) can be accomplished using any one of many methodologies. IDOV is one popular methodology for designing products and services to meet six sigma standards.

IDOV is a four-phase process that consists of Identify, Design, Optimize and Verify. These four phases parallel the four phases of the traditional Six Sigma improvement methodology, MAIC – Measure, Analyze, Improve and Control. The similarities can be seen below.

Identify Phase

The Identify phase begins the process with a formal tie of design to Voice of the Customer. This phase involves developing a team and team charter, gathering VOC, performing competitive analysis, and developing CTQs (Critical To Quality).

Crucial Steps:
1. Identify customer and product requirements
2. Establish the business case
3. Identify technical requirements (CTQ variables and specification limits)
4. Roles and responsibilities
5. Milestones

Key Tools:
1. QFD (Quality Function Deployment)

2. FMEA (Failure Means and Effects Analysis)
3. SIPOC (Supplier, Input, Product, Output, Customer product map)
4. IPDS (Integrated Product Delivery System)
5. Target Costing
6. Benchmarking

Design Phase

The Design phase emphasizes CTQs (Critical To Quality) and consists of identifying functional requirements, developing alternative concepts, evaluating alternatives and selecting a best-fit concept, deploying CTQs and predicting sigma capability.

Crucial Steps:
1. Formulate concept design
2. Identify potential risks using FMEA
3. For each technical requirement, identify design parameters (CTQs) using engineering analysis such as simulation
4. Raw materials and procurement plan
5. Manufacturing plan
6. Use DOE (design of experiments) and other analysis tools to determine CTQs and their influence on the technical requirements (transfer functions)

Key Tools:
1. Smart simple design
2. Risk assessment
3. FMEA
4. Engineering analysis
5. Materials selection software

6. Simulation
7. DOE (Design of Experiments)
8. Systems engineering
9. Analysis tools

Optimize Phase

The Optimize phase requires use of process capability information and a statistical approach to tolerancing. Developing detailed design elements, predicting performance, and optimizing design, take place within this phase.

Crucial Steps:
1. Assess process capabilities to achieve critical design parameters and meet CTQ limits
2. Optimize design to minimize sensitivity of CTQs to process parameters
3. Design for robust performance and reliability
4. Error proofing
5. Establish statistical tolerancing
6. Optimize sigma and cost
7. Commission and startup

Key Tools:
1. Manufacturing database and flow back tools
2. Design for manufacturability
3. Process capability models
4. Robust design
5. Monte Carlo Methods
6. Tolerancing
7. Six Sigma tools

Validate Phase

The Validate phase consists of testing and validating the design. As increased testing using formal tools occurs, feedback of requirements should be shared with manufacturing and sourcing, and future manufacturing and design improvements should be noted.

Crucial Steps:
1. Prototype test and validation
2. Assess performance, failure modes, reliability, and risks
3. Design iteration
4. Final phase review

Key Tools:
1. Accelerated testing
2. Reliability engineering
3. FMEA
4. Disciplined New Product Introduction (DNPI)

Tools & Templates
1. 5S
2. Affinity Diagram/KJ Analysis
3. Analysis of Variance (ANOVA)
4. Analytic Hierarchy Process (AHP)
5. Brainstorming
6. Calculators
7. Capability Indices/Process Capability

Cause & Effect
1. Control Charts

2. Design of Experiments (DOE)
3. FMEA
4. Graphical Analysis Charts
5. Hypothesis Testing
6. Kano Analysis
7. Measurement Systems Analysis (MSA)/Gage R&R

Normality
1. Pareto
2. Poka Yoke
3. Process Mapping
4. Project Charter
5. QFD/House of Quality
6. RACI Diagram
7. Regression
8. Risk Management
9. SIPOC/COPIS
10. Sampling/Data
11. Simulation
12. Software
13. Statistical Analysis
14. Surveys

Templates
1. Value Stream Mapping
2. Variation
3. Wizards

Chapter 10: Driving Lean Upstream can Multiply its Benefits

I don't mean to frighten you, but lean manufacturing initiatives may prove to be too little, too late. After all, even if your firm manages to strip every dollop of waste from the factory floor, it can still fail in the marketplace by being slow to market with inherently "fat" products. Without eliminating waste from the new product development process, the substantial benefits of lean manufacturing cannot be fully realized.

The problem is that most of the cost of a product is etched in stone long before its launch. An overly complex design, for example, cannot easily be "leaned out" in production. Moreover, unnecessary delays in product launch may cost your company unrecoverable profits. As precious weeks of profitable sales pass you by, your firm stumbles through slow decisions, changing requirements, and endless glitches prior to launch. In short, the benefits of lean manufacturing can easily be undermined by sub-optimized designs that arrive late to the factory with major engineering problems still unresolved.

It may be hard for a battle-weary change warrior such as yourself to accept this, but the holistic ideal of the lean enterprise is much more than a slightly expanded version of lean manufacturing. As challenging as a lean factory implementation can be, it is the easy part. Dramatic bottom-line results depend on eliminating waste from both the factory floor and the design process that feeds it. Whereas many firms are taking the former seriously, the vital (and often, tragically wasteful) activities that lead up to product launch have been, to date, almost completely ignored.

If you don't believe that there is a mountain of waste in your up-front design process, consider Dilbert. We all laugh at the endless frustrations and mindless quirks of the "front office" that Scott Adams has so incisively captured. Yet shouldn't we be crying? Consider the impact of such inefficiencies on your balance sheet. Recent studies of project team members have shown that in many cases, less than one hour of a typical workday is spent doing work that an outside customer would willingly pay for. How is this possible?

The answer: endless meetings, disruptive change, delayed information; lack of prioritization, poor definition of roles and responsibilities, design overshoot...the list is long and challenging.

Fortunately, the same five lean principles that have enabled monumental improvements to recurring manufacturing can guide us out of this wasteful product development miasma.

Before we charge into the engineering department with our kanban cards in hand, however, we should stop to think about the unique nature of new product development. The first and most important distinction is that product development involves two kinds of waste:

1. Waste associated with the process of creating a new design (e.g., wasted time, resources, development money), and waste that is embodied in the design itself (e.g., excessive complexity, poor manufacturing process compatibility, many unique and custom parts).
2. A second unique attribute of new product development is that the design process involves creative thinking, rather than just turning the crank. Hence, it may be difficult to just "lean it out" without risking throwing the baby out with the bath water.

Which parts of the creative process are waste and which are pure value?

The good news is that many familiar lean tools translate into new product development very nicely. Value-stream mapping and kaizen events, for example, work well in this new and challenging domain. What is fundamentally different is the toolbox. Although analogies exist between the methods of lean manufacturing and the methods of lean product development, there are fundamental differences as well. Kanban cards are replaced by linked deliverables; capacity is managed through design-specific "time slicing" techniques, and so on. New tools but a proven and well understood improvement process.

A final encouraging note is in order. The greatest single advantage of lean manufacturing methods is their almost childlike simplicity. They are typically easy to understand, straightforward to deploy, and yield unambiguous benefits.

The tools of lean product development share this user-friendly nature. They are straightforward to apply at minimal cost, and begin yielding savings the very next day. All that is required for success is a bit of organizational discipline, and an intolerance of waste in all aspects of your enterprise.

One of the best ways to achieve "balanced excellence" in product design is to focus on the elimination of non-value-added waste in both the process of development and in the design of the products themselves. To achieve this waste-slashing capability, we have adapted one of the most powerful and successful improvement philosophies of the last decade.

The principles of "lean thinking" have been strikingly successful to date at reducing waste in the manufacturing arena. Techniques such as Just-in-Time (JIT) materials management, pull systems, and batch-size reduction have enabled firms worldwide to achieve unprecedented production efficiencies. Unfortunately, a lean factory can only manufacture what it is given; if a "fat" product is handed off to the factory, all the lean manufacturing in the world won't get all of the waste out. This is where the methods of lean 3P and lean product development take centre stage.

We have therefore decided to conclude this chapter looking at lean cost reduction and lean product development. Together, they enable the elimination of waste and the enhancement of value in all aspects of product design and development.

Lean Cost Reduction / Lean 3P

This is a powerful, integrated set of team-friendly tools to slash manufacturing cost at all levels, from individual products to entire product lines.

Lean Product Development

Is a practical approach to accelerating time-to-market through aggressive waste elimination in planning, resource management, design control, and interdisciplinary communication.

What is Lean Cost Reduction / Lean 3P?

So where do you start? Naturally, your highest priorities for improvement will greatly depend on the nature of your specific market situation, but in general, cost reduction (the dimension we are calling Lean 3P) is the most logical starting point. Why? Depending on your business environment, it might be that slashing time-to-market or driving toward higher levels of innovation will give you greater overall benefit. However, reducing manufacturing cost is the fastest and surest way to achieve a measurable increase in profits. Speeding up the development process often requires disruptive changes in how a firm operates, and those changes may impact virtually everyone in the company. Moreover, the benefits won't be felt for months or years, depending on your typical development cycle-time. Cost reduction, on the other hand, can be applied to both new product ideas and existing successful products, requires minimal organizational change, and can yield immediate bottom-line results. Therefore, slashing costs is a great place to begin your journey toward lean product design excellence.

There are numerous opportunities to slash manufacturing cost during the design cycle, including:

Reduce Direct Material Cost

Common parts, common raw materials, parts-count reduction, design simplification, reduction of scrap and quality defects, elimination of batch processes, etc.

Reduce Direct Labour Cost

Design simplification, design for lean manufacture and assembly, parts count reduction, matching product tolerances to process capabilities, standardizing processes, etc.

Reduce Operational Overhead

Minimize impact on factory layout, capture cross-product-line synergies (e.g. a modular design/mass-customization strategy), improve utilization of shared capital equipment, etc.

Minimize Non-Recurring Design Cost

Platform design strategies, parts standardization, lean QFD/voice-of-the-customer, Six-Sigma Methods, Design of Experiment, Value Engineering, Production Preparation (3P) Process, etc.

Minimize Product-Specific Capital Investment

Production Preparation (3P) Process, matching product tolerances to process capabilities, Value Engineering / design simplification, design for one-piece flow, standardization of parts, etc.

Chapter 11: Myths and Misconceptions about DFSS

One common misconception about DFSS is that it's a replacement for your current new product development process. If no formal process exists within your company, it could be used to guide the development process, but typically DFSS provides the tools, teamwork, and data to supplement the new product development process already in place in an organization.

Another misconception is that DFSS is just Six Sigma in design. The truth, simply put it, is that DFSS is a complex methodology of systems engineering analysis that uses statistical methods.

Related beliefs are that DFSS is just Design for Manufacturability and Assembly (DFMA) and/or Design of Experiments (DOE) and Robust Design concepts in engineering. Those beliefs are based on an overly simplified understanding of DFSS. It's actually a comprehensive process that involves DFMA issues and applies DOE and Robust Design among many methods. Because of its use of statistical methods, people may believe that DFSS demands extensive statistical analysis and modelling of all requirements. This is untrue.

DFSS calls for dealing with each engineering requirement optimally. Consequently, some requirements are analyzed statistically but some requirements are handled with traditional engineering methods.

Another misconception is that DFSS allows too much design margin, so that costs are higher, and/or increases development cycle times, so that market opportunities are missed. In fact, however, DFSS balances cost, cycle times and schedule, and quality.

Some people think of DFSS as being simply a collection of tools. This is a misunderstanding. Although DFSS uses some powerful tools, those tools alone will not ensure success, not unless those using them know how to apply them to specific engineering design opportunities.

Another misconception is that DFSS involves just the core product design team and has no impact on marketing, research, and manufacturing. Because of tools recently added to DFSS, this is no longer true. The most effective product development teams are cross-functional, with strong project management leadership and management support. Marketing, research, design, and advanced manufacturing engineering are typical representatives in a DFSS wave. The team works together to scope customer requirements, select design concepts, detail the product and process design, select suppliers, and ensure that supplier capability meets or exceeds customer driven engineering needs.

One comment that we hear is that DFSS may apply to many engineering disciplines, but not to all. However, since DFSS is not specific to any discipline, it applies to all. The analysis will differ according to the discipline, but most of the DFSS principles will apply.

Another misconception is that all management needs to do is "sign the cheque" and DFSS will happen overnight. Management must play an important role in leading the change effort. Activities such as linking the DFSS process with the company vision, establishing an executive change council to drive implementation, making successes visible, guiding implementation throughout the organization, and making DFSS integral to the company culture are all vital.

Another misconception involves classroom training. Training in tools with no implementation plan does not result in cultural change. Far too many organizations develop or purchase extensive training initiatives, train employees in a classroom environment, and expect implementation to just happen. Classroom training that is not integral to implementation does not work. Another approach is just-in-time training. Team members learn about a tool as they need it; initial facilitation support is provided as they learn how to apply the tool and simultaneously work on the new product.

Chapter 12: Question Time!

What is DFSS?

DFSS stands for Design For Six Sigma; an approach to designing or re-designing a new product and/or service for a commercial market, with a measurably high process-sigma for performance from day one. The intension of DFSS is to bring such new products and/or services to market with a process performance of around 4.5 sigma or better, for every customer requirement. This implies an ability to understand the customer needs and to design and implement the new offering with a reliability of delivery before launch rather than after!

Is DFSS a methodology?

Not really. DFSS is an approach and attitude towards delivering new products and services with a high performance as measured by customer critical to quality metrics. Just as the Six Sigma approach has the DMAIC methodology (Define, Measure, Analyse, Improve, Control) by which processes can be improved, DFSS also has a methodology by which new products and services can be designed and implemented.

DMAIC is now an industry standard methodology for Six Sigma; however DFSS does not yet have such a universal offering. DMADV (Design, Measure, Analyse, Design, Verify) is one approach; however there are several in use. In many engineering design departments, DFSS is regarded as design optimisation, and the IDOV (Identify, Design, Optimise, Verify) methodology prevails, however this is focused very much on final stage engineering optimisation, and may miss many of the issues involved in actually selecting good products and features that will meet customer needs!

To deliver a good methodology that is customer focused, encompasses the entire business-to-market process, and deals effectively with both products and services, Geoff Tennant uses the DCCDI methodology - Define, Customer, Concept, Design, Implement.

What are the differences between Six Sigma and DFSS?

Six Sigma is a process improvement philosophy and methodology, whereas DFSS is centred on designing new products and services. The main differences are that Six Sigma focuses on one or two CTQ (Critical To Quality) metrics, looks at processes, and aims to improve the CTQ performance by about +1 process-sigma. In contrast, DFSS focuses on every single CTQ that matters to every customer, looks at products and services as well as the processes by which they are delivered, and aims to bring forth a new product/service with a performance of about 4.5 sigma or better.

Other differences are that DFSS projects are often much larger and take longer, and are often based on a long term business need for new products, rather than a short term need to fix a customer problem.

In practicality the divide between a formal DFSS project and a 'simple' Six Sigma project can be indistinct at times there is a need for a Six Sigma project to radically improve the capability (rather than, or as well as, performance) of a broken or non-existent process using design or re-design.

Is DFSS only for manufacturing design?

Certainly not! Design traditionally has been associated with products much more than for services, however this is changing as companies realise that every product has associated services, many of which may matter more to the customer than the product! Engineers may be interested in using some of the 'six sigma' tools such as DOE (Design Of Experiments) to 'micro-optimise' design parameters. This runs the risk of turning out a perfect design but failing to deliver to all the customer requirements or a real commercial and business need. A full approach to DFSS will consider every aspect from the business NPI (New Product Introduction) strategy right through to ongoing commercialization. Any good DFSS methodology and approach must work as a framework for any type of design and for both products and services.

Where can I use DFSS in my company?

DFSS can be used anywhere a new product or service is to be introduced or re-introduced. For many manufacturing organisations the design and development of new products is very much a part of everyday company life, and a soundly adopted DFSS methodology can make a considerable improvement to the process of 'design and implement'.

Design and re-design can occur within any standard DMAIC project, and since there are many degrees of design within many commercial environments, there will be many 'flavours' of DFSS. These range from very large projects involving major design of entirely new and complex product/services, through to small 'excursions' into DFSS from a DMAIC type project.

Large DFSS projects are best suited for the introduction of new products/services with major design and large impact, and where customer approval and high levels of performance and delivery are required. DFSS is about reducing the risk of failure; failure to promote and develop the correct products/services, failure to identify all the customers and customer requirements, failure to design and implement appropriately and without error or omission.

What are the main tools used in DFSS?

It is very important to have practical experience of Six Sigma, as DFSS builds on the concepts and tools from a typical DMAIC approach. Since DFSS works with products/services rather than processes, and since design and creativity are important, a few new tools are common to any DFSS methodology. Strong emphasis is placed on customer analysis, the transition of customer needs and requirements (of the product/service) down to process requirements, and on error and failure proofing. Since the product/service is often very new, modelling and simulation tools are important, particularly for measuring and evaluating in advance the anticipated performance of the new process.

The main tools include QFD - Quality Function Deployment, FMEA - Failure Mode Effect Analysis, DOE - Design Of Experiment, and simulation techniques. However, just as in Six Sigma, the ability of the approach to be successful in use does not depend entirely on the tools used. Six Sigma brings a methodology (DMAIC) as well as a wider, deeper and more integrated use of existing tools. DFSS methodologies are about a wider, deeper and more integrated approach to commercial design, which involves everyone in the process as well as the customer to deliver a better product/service and final implementation!

What is the correct order for using these tools?

If DFSS is to work successfully, it is important that it covers the full life-cycle of any new product or service. This begins when the organisation formally agrees the requirement for something new, and ends when the new product/service is in full commercial delivery.

Chapter 13: New Product Introduction

The start of the DFSS project for real. Plenty more benchmarking, customer survey and analysis, and more work on a team charter to build a solid foundation for the project.

Customer (Measure)

The stage where the customers are fully identified and their needs collected and analysed. Mostly work with Quality Function Deployment (QFD) but here the aim is to identify the most appropriate set of CTQ (Critical To Quality) metrics to use to measure and evaluate the design by. This comes from a set of customer needs, together with a list of potential measures, and a lot of work on the first 'house of quality'. Hopefully too the start of numerical limits and targets for each CTQ!

Concept (Analyse - conceptual design)

The team take the concept provided by the business for the new product/service and begin to flesh out the concept to a working 'paper design'. This will require 'non-technical' design and a second round of QFD to identify the best 'features' that have the potential to deliver to the CTQs. Here we begin to move from CTQ to CTP - Critical To Process metrics. The idea is that, if the process by which the product/service is manufactured/delivered is 100%, then the product/service will also deliver to the customer CTQs and hence deliver to all of the customer needs! The end of this stage is a set of design concepts together with a set of CTPs that will constrain the formal and technical design.

Design (technical design)

The team handover the 'design brief' and the designers then complete the work, using all the CTPs as guides and evaluators to ensure that the design is perfect! Technical design can be carried out by the project team for simpler and service-type design, or by more technical and perhaps traditional design methods for more complex situations. Here we can use DOE and other statistical optimisation techniques, as well as greater creativity to bring inspired solutions that are proven to deliver. Simulation of both product, service and process are important tools.

Implement

No product or service should go directly to market without first piloting and refining. Here the team can use Failure Mode Effect Analysis (FMEA) as well as pilot and small scale implementations to test and evaluate real-life performance. Note however that this should be a fine tuning exercise and not a total re-design at this stage! Full scale commercial rollout will often then follow.

Handover

Once fully implemented, the new product/service and supporting processes can be handed over to (new) process owners, complete with new CTQs and monitoring systems! Naturally we have omitted to mention good amounts of project management, risk analysis and sound communication, as well as teamwork!

Chapter 14: Conclusion

The entire Design for Six Sigma – DFSS - is an upcoming and isolated business procedure of regulation of Six Sigma's doctrine. There are several tools and methods to utilize within Six Sigma for the process to be running in the correct direction and DFSS has the methods to determine the need of the business and customers. This process is very essential to the business because of their relevant process.

The relevant process of DFSS or design for Six Sigma includes an intricate data phase that is continued through a developed system. Generation becomes more of the process than improvement. Generation meaning an attempt to avoid unnecessary processes and to use different systems in order to reach the conclusion. This is all in hopes of bettering the company quickly.

The original process that is typically practiced and used through different solving tools is DMAIC. The phases of this process include define, measure, analyze, improve, and control. These tools are used to remove defects and find other issues that are involved with the defects to remove those. As soon, as the defects are found, they begin a process to ensure that the situation does not occur again or is further induced. However, design for this company has gradually graduated towards something bigger.

This type of system attempts to bring into existence an entire new process, through an entire new means of research, since none before existed. This was created in place for the present system that was no longer adequate and needed to be reinvented. The main objective of the system is to create a process that betters the doctrine of Six Sigma before it is initiated.

In the beginning, the original process sought after continual improvement once a process had existed. This attempts to improve the process and ameliorate it before the process has begun. This has been a new approach to design and avoids service process issues by utilizing new and improved Voice Customer tactics.

In this manner, any engineering tactics can be used to increase the service efficiency in the eye of the client. Through the engineering process, they attempt to provide satisfaction for their customers and increase the share of the market. The process is extensive and does include the ability to predict, model, simulate, train, and analyze, in order to create the best product and service for the customer.

There have been several comments about the practices used by the engineering and the design quality. Many individuals wonder just how unique the product is and what it provides on a daily basis. However, DFSS, or design for six sigma, is taking that and creating new face value and attempting to please the suppliers, and clients while maintaining its creative yet, effective development process. Here, product has been designed to become a modification for the company that could function at any level of performance. The product can also be used to create processes without engineering.

Each and every business process presents an opportunity for a variation to occur. The likelihood for the occurrence of a deviation is especially high when the process involves human operations. It goes without saying that each deviation can potentially become a defect, one that would need additional costs for it to be corrected. It is because of this that the Design for Six Sigma - DFSS is important for every business.

Theoretically, the six sigma status would mean less than 3.4 failures per a million attempts. Although this is a very low failure rate, it has been proven achievable when the tenets of the Design for Six Sigma - DFSS are implemented as required. There are two main aspects to this approach, managing company resources and meeting customer expectations by delivering superior quality products. DFSS is a formal set of project management techniques and theories that need to be applied to the business management operations of a company. The techniques are simply guidelines for how a company ought to manufacture its products and create its services in a perfect world.

Client management is a key aspect when it comes to the design for six sigma. It is easily accomplished by ensuring verification and quality measures are taken into consideration right from the inception of a service or product development, to see to it that customer needs and expectations are met. This is what is referred to as Quality Function Development (QFD), a formal way of transforming a business need into a practical process.

The term failure is clearly defined within each of the industries where this formula for success is applied, and in every product line. Failure simply means a fault that consumers consider critical. There are two major methodologies used today. The first one is the DMAIC process, which stands for define, measure, analyze, improve, and control. DMADV is the second process, and stands for define, measure, analyze, design, and verify.

The first methodology, DMAIC, is applicable in processes that are already implemented but do not meet the specifications recommended. It is used to help upgrade the already running processes up to the recommended threshold. The second methodology, DMADV, is applicable in the development of new services or products, to help ensure they meet the recommended levels of quality.

The values of the Design for Six Sigma - DFSS are straight forward and very useful and practical for companies and businesses of all sizes. By relentlessly channelling all efforts towards quality and reducing defects and variations in the consistency of services or products, the values recommended guarantee a better business, one that is able to achieve its best possible bottom line more easily.

Sometimes when a company tries to become "lean" or wants to improve time to market with defect free product or service and become more efficient, the company will start to introduce numerous concepts developed by Toyota and others. The problem is that a company does not know the order in which to implement the dfss changes or why they should implement what they are implementing. This approach greatly slows design and new product introduction improvements when complementary or contradictive concepts are introduced on an ad-hoc basis.

Understanding the needs of the customer for a particular market segment is critical to success. We must get it right in this important first stage. All too often, however, this does not happen. Far too often, organizations do little more than review complaints and simply ask the customers what new features they would like to have added to the product. That's valuable, of course, but it's not going far enough.

Focus groups and interviews can also provide valuable information about the customer, but many times respondents offer feedback couched in terms of technical solutions.

Customers offer technical solutions because they believe this is the best solution they're aware of. For example, they may want a laptop computer with a 140 GB disk drive, but what is their underlying need? Do they want faster boot-up time, storage space for pictures, audio, video? It's far better for the design team to understand the latent underlying need and then allow the technical arm of the design team to determine the best technical solution. Enough said!

Good Luck!

Made in the USA
Lexington, KY
23 September 2015